The Ultimate Self-Teaching Method! Level Two

•Play
Violin
Today!

A Complete Guide to the Basics

Recorded and Produced by Dan Maske
Violin by Jerry Loughney

PLAYBACK+
Speed • Pitch • Balance • Loop

To access audio visit:
www.halleonard.com/mylibrary

Enter Code
2038-4322-8668-9613

ISBN: 978-1-4234-9434-8

Visit Hal Leonard Online at
www.halleonard.com

Contact Us:
Hal Leonard
7777 West Bluemound Road
Milwaukee, WI 53213
Email: info@halleonard.com

In Europe contact:
Hal Leonard Europe Limited
42 Wigmore Street
Marylebone, London, W1U 2RN
Email: info@halleonardeurope.com

In Australia contact:
Hal Leonard Australia Pty. Ltd.
4 Lentara Court
Cheltenham, Victoria, 3192 Australia
Email: info@halleonard.com.au

Introduction

Track 1

Welcome back to *Play Violin Today!* The exercises and pieces in Level Two will help develop your technique, range, and musical abilities. With practice and by following all the suggestions in this book you will grow in your abilities as a violinist.

About the Audio

The accompanying audio will make your learning even more enjoyable, as we take you step by step through each lesson and play each song along with a full band. Much as a real lesson, the best way to learn this material is to read and practice a while first on your own, then listen to the recording. With *Play Violin Today! Level Two*, you learn at your own pace. If there is ever something that you don't understand the first time through, go back to the recording and listen again. Every musical track has been given a track number, so if you want to practice a song again, you can find it right away. You may remove the violin from the recording by turning down the right channel to play along with the accompaniment only.

Contents

A Quick Review

Holding Your Violin

With the left hand, pick up your violin by the neck with the strings facing away from you. Hold the instrument where the neck meets the body. If you grab it too close to the pegs, you may "bump" them, throwing the instrument out of tune.

Turn the violin toward you, with the strings facing the ceiling. Bring the violin to your left shoulder placing the side of your left jaw against the chin rest, creating a slight angle between your face and the violin, with the violin angling to the left.

Although it is called a chin rest, your chin never rests directly on the chin rest, rather your jaw is what comes most in contact with it. Slide your left hand toward the pegs, stopping about 1 1/2 inches in front of the nut. Curve your fingers slightly around the neck to touch the strings. Your thumb remains unbent, resting against the left side of the neck. Your left hand cradles the neck in this way, however it does not support the weight of your instrument. Your shoulder and chin support and hold the instrument. Your left wrist should be straight, and your left arm and elbow should be directly beneath the middle of the violin. Practice holding the violin under your chin without your left hand for

several seconds, gradually adding to the amount of time you can support the violin without your left hand. Try to keep your neck and shoulder as relaxed as possible while still supporting the weight of the violin. You may find that a soft sponge or shoulder rest attached beneath the violin will help cushion the space between the violin and your shoulder. This can help make holding the violin more comfortable.

The Bow

Preparing Your Bow

When a bow is stored in its case, the hair is loosened. After taking the bow from your case to play, you will need to tighten the hair by turning the screw clockwise, until the hair is straight and firm, still leaving the stick visibly bowed. Take care not to over tighten the hair, which could damage the bow and produce a harsh sound.

Before playing, rosin the bow by holding the rosin in your left hand while sliding the bow back and forth across the rosin, moving the bow and holding the rosin steady. You will need to apply a little rosin each time you take your violin out to play.

Remember to loosen the bow hair by turning the screw counterclockwise before putting the bow back in the case again.

Holding the Bow

As you learn to hold the bow for the first time, put down your violin so your left hand can assist you. As you become more comfortable with your bow, you will be able to pick it up easily with your right hand alone.

Using your left hand, pick up the bow in the middle of the stick with the hair facing the floor. You should always avoid touching the hair. Place the tip of your right thumb against the spot where the left end of the frog meets the stick, bending your thumb joint slightly.

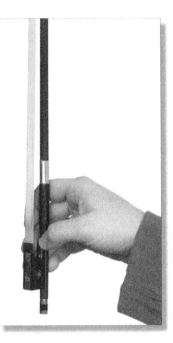

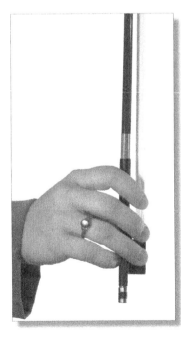

Allow your middle and ring fingers to curve over the stick – your middle finger roughly opposite your thumb, touching the ferrule. The first joint of your index finger will rest along the top of the stick in the middle of the winding, and the tip of your little finger will rest on top of the stick near the screw. Your hand should be relaxed with the fingers spread comfortably. You will want to practice finding this position several times each day until it becomes easy.

The hair should still be facing the floor. Carefully let go of the stick with your left hand. You will notice the weighty feeling on the frog side of the bow.

Learning to properly hold the bow takes a little patience and practice. As you begin to learn notes on the violin, you may wish to pluck the string first, instead of using the bow right away. Plucking a stringed instrument is called "pizzicato." As you play new notes and pieces pizzicato, continue to practice holding the bow to become more comfortable with it.

Tuning Your Violin

The four strings on the violin are tuned to the following pitches, from bottom (low) to top (high): G, D, A, E.

You can adjust each pitch by tightening or loosening each string by turning its corresponding peg. You can make very small adjustments to the string by turning the fine tuners. To tune your violin it is easiest to use an electronic tuner or a piano or keyboard. You may also use a pitch pipe or tuning fork. Track 6 will also enable you to tune your violin. Always tune your instrument before playing.

Violin Care Tip

When placing the violin back in its case, always wipe the rosin off the strings with a soft cloth. This will ensure a longer string life. Also, to protect the wood of the instrument, it is good to place a humidifier in the case during the colder months of the year. Ask for a violin humidifier at your local music store.

Tuning the A string:

Place your violin in playing position with your bow. Listen to the A on the recording, electric tuner, or piano. Play the A on your violin to determine if it matches the A being played. Raise the pitch by turning the corresponding peg slowly and carefully *away* from you. Lower the pitch by turning the peg slowly and carefully *toward* you. If the pitch is very close, use the fine tuner to a make a smaller adjustment. (Not all violins come equipped with fine tuners on all four strings. As a beginner, it is recommended you have a fine tuner on each string.) Turning the fine tuner clockwise **raises** the pitch, counterclockwise **lowers** the pitch. Continue tuning the other three strings in the same manner. The tuning notes are played in the order: A–D–G–E.

Some Tuning Tips:

While tightening or loosening a string, turn the peg or fine tuner slowly, concentrating on the changes in pitch. You might need to pluck the string repeatedly to compare the sound of your string to the note you are tuning to.

As you're tuning a string, you may notice a series of pulsating beat waves. These beat waves can help you tune; they'll slow down as the pitches get closer together, stopping completely when the two pitches are the same, meaning they are in tune.

Instead of tuning a string down to a pitch, tune it up. This allows you to stretch the string into place, which will help it stay in tune longer. If a string is too high in pitch, tune it down first, then bring it back up to pitch. Always be careful not to tune a string too high or too quickly. Strings can break easily as a result, especially the E string.

Note Review and New Rhythm

The following chart will help you review the notes you learned in *Play Violin Today! Level One*.

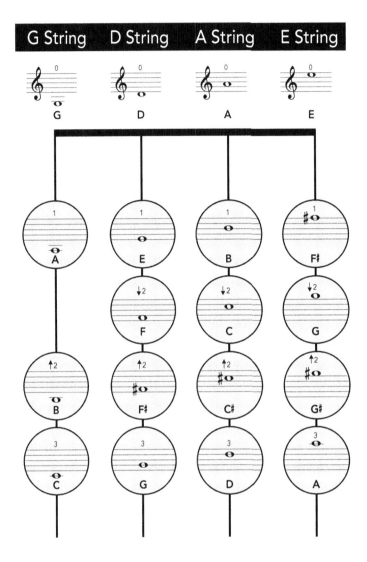

For each musical example, note the key signature and the time signature. Tap the rhythm of each example, and then play *pizzicato* (plucking) the first time, and *arco* (with the bow) the second time.

Track 7

Easy on the D String

Track 8

Major or Minor?

Quick Warm-up

Track 9

G String Waltz

Track 10

"Sandy Land" is a well-known American folk tune. Note the key signature, and play *pizzicato*. All the notes for "Sandy Land" are played on only two strings. Which two strings will you play?

Sandy Land

Track 11

Place your bow on the D string about two inches from the frog in order to play a short up bow as you begin "I Gave My Love a Cherry," with a quarter note pick-up. Use smooth, legato bow strokes for a flowing feel, keeping the bow moving through the half and dotted half notes.

I Gave My Love a Cherry

Track 12

New Rhythm: Dotted Quarter Note

A dot following a note adds half the note's value.

This rhythm: could also be notated using

a dot as:

In $\frac{4}{4}$ time, a dotted quarter note gets one and a half beats.

Single eighth notes are flagged instead of beamed: ← flag

Track 13

Practice tapping and counting the rhythm in "Open String Dots." When you are comfortable with the rhythm, try playing this song, first without listening to the recording. Then, listen to Track 14 to see if you played the rhythm correctly, and finally play along with the track.

Track 14

► Write in the counting for the remainder of this song using measures 1–4 as an example.

Open String Dots

Look for the dotted rhythms in the Jamaican tune, "Water Come a Me Eye." Tap or clap the first measure. Compare lines one and two: Are they exactly the same? Now compare lines three and four. The form of this piece is "AB." Knowing the form will help you learn the piece more easily.

Track 15

► Note the slurs under each group of eighth notes and remember that the slur indicates that both notes will be played in one bow stroke, in this case, a down bow.

Water Come A Me Eye

Lively   Jamaican

Test Yourself!

Divide the following rhythms into measures by drawing bar lines using the time signatures given. Then, tap and count the rhythms. You may also experiment by playing these rhythms on your violin. Use just one note or attempt to make up your own melody!

Staccato and Dynamics

Before tackling the new tunes in Chapter Two, warm up slowly with the following exercises using eighth notes. Listen for smooth and even eighths, and in variations one and two, pay close attention to the slurred bowing. To slur two eighth notes, divide your bow stroke into two equal parts. To slur four eighth notes, divide the bow into four parts.

Track 16

Eight to the Bar

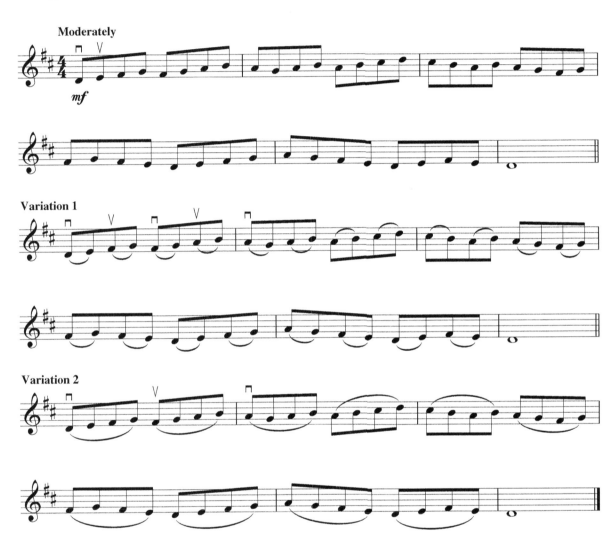

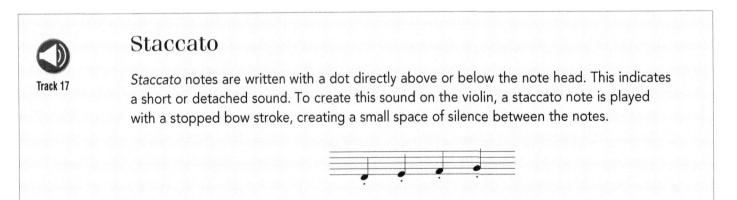

Track 17

Staccato

Staccato notes are written with a dot directly above or below the note head. This indicates a short or detached sound. To create this sound on the violin, a staccato note is played with a stopped bow stroke, creating a small space of silence between the notes.

Stopping for Staccato

Track 18

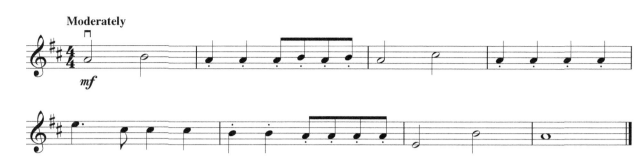

Staccato notes give "Theme from Symphony No. 94" a light-hearted and humorous feel. Use just a small amount of bow for each stopped bow stroke when playing *staccato*.

Theme from Symphony No. 94

Track 19

▶ Remember to lift your bow where indicated in order to prepare for another down bow on the next note.

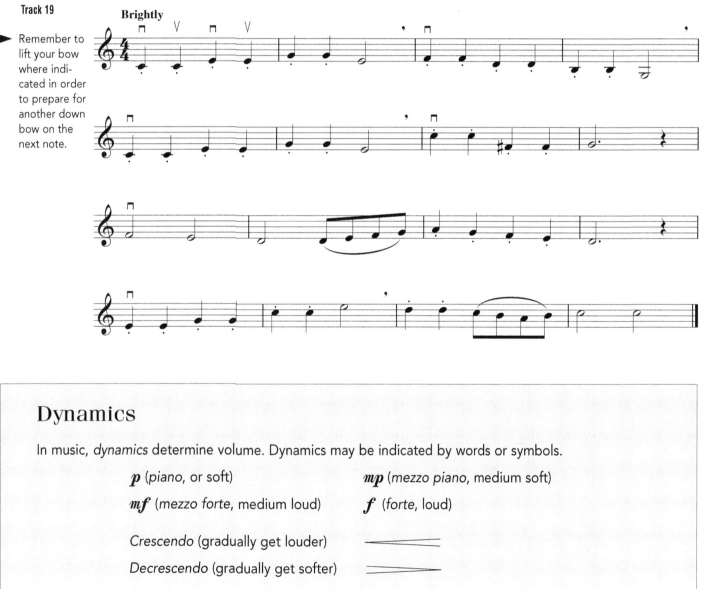

Dynamics

In music, *dynamics* determine volume. Dynamics may be indicated by words or symbols.

p (piano, or soft)   *mp* (mezzo piano, medium soft)

mf (mezzo forte, medium loud)   *f* (forte, loud)

Crescendo (gradually get louder)

Decrescendo (gradually get softer)

Before playing "Father Put the Cow Out," look through the piece and note the many dynamic changes. Play with more weight in the bow for a louder sound, and less weight for a softer sound.

Track 20

Father Put the Cow Out

American

► Notice how measures 9–10 are *staccato*, but 11–12 are not. Work on making a difference in the style between these two groups of measures.

"Long, Long Ago" is a well-known tune with a beautiful flowing melody. Practice the crescendo and decrescendo until you achieve the sound you desire. Keep the bow moving through the notes to produce a singing legato tone. In the last measure, the fermata sign ⌢ indicates that you may hold the last note as long as you wish.

Track 21

Long, Long Ago

T. H. Bayly

Track 22

Lesson 3 | A New Scale

Track 23

Playing the G Major Scale

A major scale consists of eight notes in the following pattern of whole and half steps:

Starting note–W–W–H–W–W–W–H

Beginning on G, following this pattern of half and whole steps gives us the notes
G–A–B–C–D–E–F♯–G.

Playing major scales are a great warm-up, and are beneficial to understanding fingering patterns.

Play the following two-octave G major scale with detached bowing, changing the bow stroke
on every note. You may also play the scale *pizzicato*. Listen carefully for accurate intonation.

Track 24

G Major Scale

Track 25

Chords and Arpeggios

A *chord* consists of three or more notes played at the same time or *harmonically*. The notes of
a chord are often the interval of a third apart, as in the following G chord:

Chords are most often played on instruments such as piano or guitar.

An *arpeggio* (sometimes referred to as a "broken chord") is a chord with the notes played one
at a time or *melodically*. A G major chord would consist of the first, third, and fifth notes of the
G major scale.

Playing *arpeggios* is an excellent way to work on accurate intonation. Play the following *arpeggio* using the notes from the G major scale.

Track 26

G Arpeggio

Track 27

Notice the musical signs above measures 4–5, and 6–7 in the next piece, "St. Anthony Chorale." These are called *first* and *second endings*. After playing measures 4–5 (first ending) follow the repeat sign back to the beginning, but this time, after playing measure 3, skip to the second ending to play measures 6–7.

Track 28

St. Anthony Chorale

F. J. Haydn

Track 29

Hooked Bowing

Hooked bowing is when two (or more) notes are played in the same direction with a stop in the motion of the bow between the notes, notated like this:

Practice hooked bowing as you play "By Hook or by Crook." The quarter notes will have short, stopped bow strokes.

Track 30

By Hook or By Crook

Track 31

"Theme from Symphony No. 9" uses a dotted rhythm throughout. Clap and count this rhythm, then play the notes *pizzicato* to become familiar with this famous tune. When you're ready to use the bow, notice that a hooked bowing is used to connect the dotted quarter and eighth notes. Remember to use a longer stroke for the dotted quarter, and a short stroke for the eighth note.

Track 32

Theme from Symphony No. 9

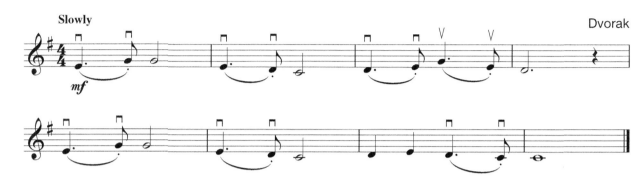

Track 33

Johann Sebastian Bach (1685–1750) is a well-known composer from the Baroque period. He wrote many works for string instruments, as well as for woodwind, voice, and keyboard. "Minuet" is a slow and graceful dance in $\frac{3}{4}$ time. Use a hooked bowing in the first measure as indicated. Listen to the dance-like rhythmic feel which should result from playing the repeated notes bowed in this way.

Track 34

Minuet

New Note on the D String

Track 35

New Note: A on the D String

Placing the fourth finger on a string matches the pitch of the next highest open string. For example, finger 4 on the D string is the same pitch as the open A string.

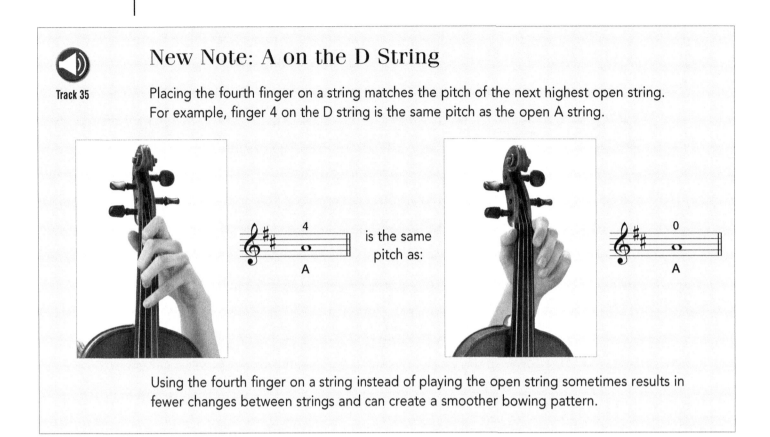

Using the fourth finger on a string instead of playing the open string sometimes results in fewer changes between strings and can create a smoother bowing pattern.

By using finger 4 on the D string, "Ode to Joy" can be played entirely on one string.

Track 36

Ode to Joy

"German Folk Song" can also be played entirely on the D string.

Track 37

German Folk Song

German

Play the D major scale below. Notice that A is played as an open string going up the scale (ascending), but is played with finger 4 on the D string going down the scale (descending).

Track 38

D Major Scale

Try the same fingering when playing the D major *arpeggio*. Play open A when ascending, then finger 4 on the D string when descending.

Track 39

D Major Arpeggio

"French Folk Song" is a lovely flowing tune. Use plenty of bow on the repeated notes for a smooth *legato* sound, and pay special care to the dynamics marked.

Track 40

French Folk Song

French

▶ Experiment by adding your own bowings such as hooked bowings on repeated notes and additional slurs. Pencil in your new bowings and use them to help play the song more expressively.

Test Yourself!

Name the string and finger number you would use to play the notes given. Example one is done for you.

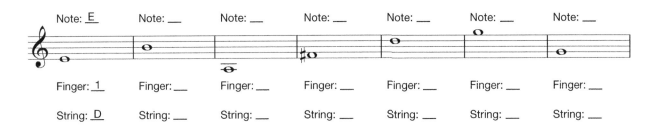

Note: E Note: __ Note: __ Note: __ Note: __ Note: __ Note: __

Finger: 1 Finger: __ Finger: __ Finger: __ Finger: __ Finger: __ Finger: __

String: D String: __ String: __ String: __ String: __ String: __ String: __

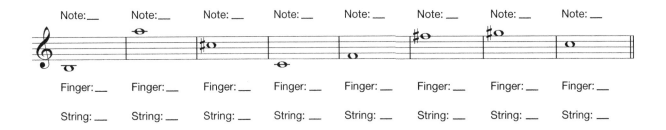

Note: __ Note: __ Note: __ Note: __ Note: __ Note: __ Note: __ Note: __

Finger: __ Finger: __ Finger: __ Finger: __ Finger: __ Finger: __ Finger: __ Finger: __

String: __ String: __ String: __ String: __ String: __ String: __ String: __ String: __

New Note on the G String

Track 41

New Note: D on the G String

Remembering that finger 4 on a string sounds the same as the next open string higher, we can play D by using finger 4 on the G string. As you reach across with finger 4, remember to keep your hand relaxed and your elbow directly under the body of your violin.

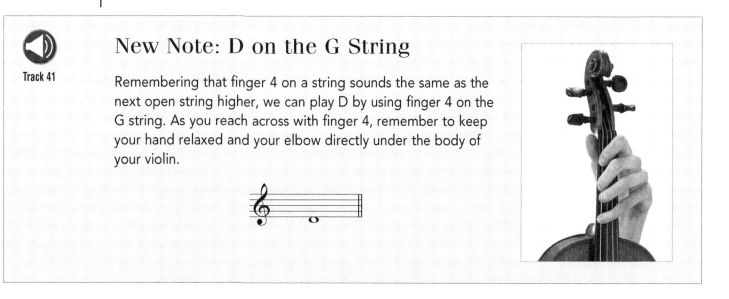

As you play "Delightfully D" listen for the G-string D and the open-string D to sound the same.

Track 42

Delightfully D

Track 43

The key of C major has no sharps or flats in the key signature. Play the following scales and *arpeggios* with precise eighth-note rhythms. Play at a slow tempo first, and then challenge yourself by increasing the tempo while keeping the eighth notes steady. You may wish to use a metronome to assist you.

Track 44

► In addition to playing the dynamics as written, try the opposite: begin *forte* and *decrescendo* during the first line, then *crescendo* on the second line, ending *forte*.

C Major Scale

C Major Arpeggio

Track 45

Watch for slurs as you play "Yankee Doodle." Notice that all of the Ds are played on the open string except for the last D in measure 15. Work toward a lively and spirited tempo.

Yankee Doodle

Track 46

American

Track 47

In the Russian folk song "Come Beautiful May," be sure to lift your bow at the rest in measure 2, and play measure 3 softly, like an echo. The D in the next to the last measure will be played with finger 4 on the G string.

Come Beautiful May

Track 48

Russian folk song

Test Yourself!

Can you complete the following tunes? Use your ears and fingers to guide you as you hum or sing along. Attempt to play the missing notes on your violin, and when you think you have it, write the notes in the empty measures.

Alouette

London Bridge

Oh, Susanna

A Major Scale and Arpeggio

The key of A major has three sharps: F♯, C♯, and G♯. The following scale exercise asks you to slur two notes to a bow and then four notes to a bow. Be patient as you practice dividing the bow equally between the notes.

Track 49

A Major Scale

Slurring *arpeggios* is a bit trickier, but you can do it! Play slowly, concentrating on good intonation, string crossing, and the speed of your bow.

Track 50

Arpeggios to Slur

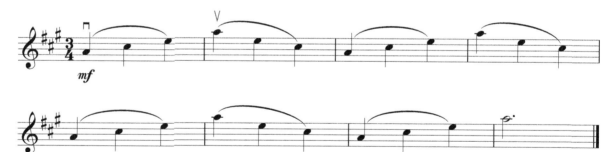

Track 51

New Note: B on the E String

Fourth finger on the E string extends our note range by a whole step. Listen carefully to keep the new note, B, in tune.

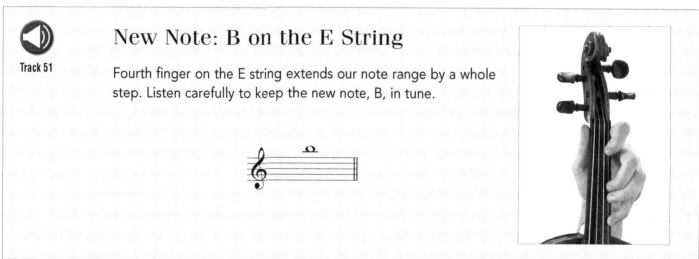

Easy Does It

The American folk song "Sourwood Mountain" is a traditional old-time dance tune dating back to the early 1900s, originating in the southern mountain region. Try to capture some dance-like energy as you play this tune handed down from generation to generation.

Sourwood Mountain

American

▶ Notice that the dynamics change when you take the repeats. Try to make a noticeable dynamic contrast.

"Arkansas Traveler" is another traditional fiddle tune. First play it *pizzicato* to familiarize yourself with the melody. When playing it *arco*, play the tune slowly at first, paying close attention to the bowing marked. Then, increase to a lively dance tempo.

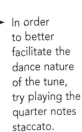

Arkansas Traveler

American

▶ In order to better facilitate the dance nature of the tune, try playing the quarter notes staccato.

Also known as "Simple Gifts," "Shaker Melody" originated in the mid 1800s as a dance tune. It became widely known after the composer Aaron Copland (1900-1990) used the melody in his famous orchestral work *Appalachian Spring*. More recently, this tune was featured in "Air and Simple Gifts" by John Williams (b. 1932), and was played at the inauguration of U.S. President Barack Obama. Play this tune with a moderate tempo and smooth bow strokes.

Shaker Melody

New G and A String Notes

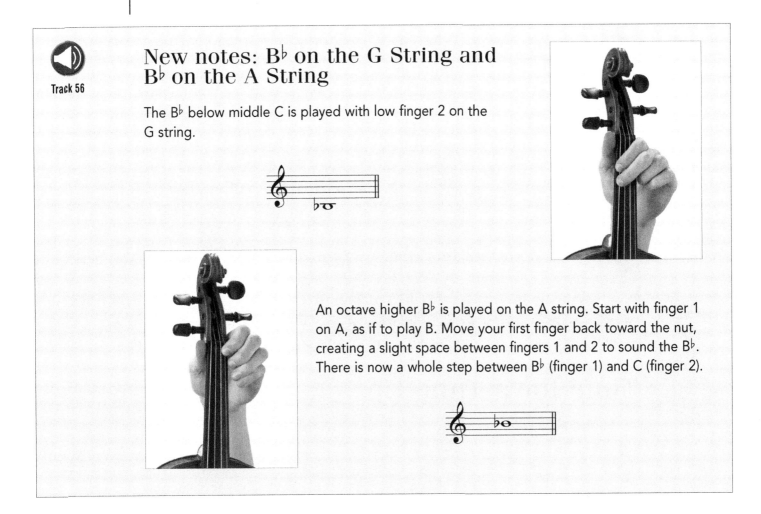

Track 56

New notes: B♭ on the G String and B♭ on the A String

The B♭ below middle C is played with low finger 2 on the G string.

An octave higher B♭ is played on the A string. Start with finger 1 on A, as if to play B. Move your first finger back toward the nut, creating a slight space between fingers 1 and 2 to sound the B♭. There is now a whole step between B♭ (finger 1) and C (finger 2).

Listen for the darker, minor sound in "Unhappy Camper" which uses the low B♭ on the G string.

Track 57

Unhappy Camper

Listen for the whole step in "Interval Waltz" which makes use of the higher B♭, on the G string.

Track 58

Interval Waltz

Track 59

All string players strive for accurate intonation. A great way to practice this is to work on matching intervals. "Time for a Tune-Up" includes major, minor, and perfect intervals.

Track 60

Time for a Tune-Up

► Listen carefully to the half-step difference between intervals such as D–F compared to D–F♯.

Note the bowing pattern at the beginning of "Kum Ba Yah." Keep the bow moving slowly and steadily as you play. This will produce a smooth, legato sound, and give you plenty of bow for the whole notes.

Track 61

Kum Ba Yah

African

Track 62

Plan ahead for the G♯ in measure 2 of "Brightness of My Day." You may wish to play this tune *pizzicato* first to practice the difference between G and G♯. Count carefully, and look out for the ties across the bar line.

Track 63

Brightness of My Day

Another tune with long bows is "Down in the Valley." As this is a slow waltz, you will need a long, slow bow to play the tied dotted half notes. Use the rests to breathe and lift the bow, starting each new phrase with a down bow.

Track 64

Down in the Valley

American

Test Yourself!

Name the following intervals in the key of G major. Sing the intervals, and then play them.

2nd

New Note on the E String

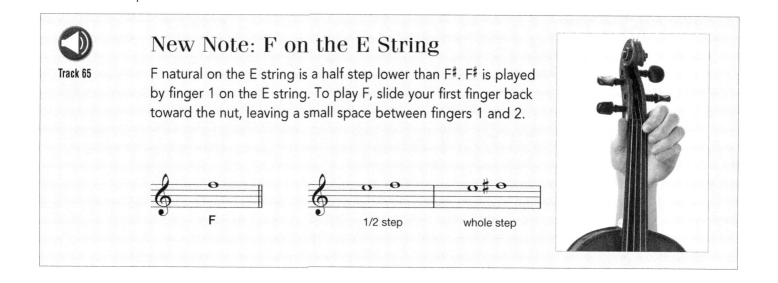

Track 65

New Note: F on the E String

F natural on the E string is a half step lower than F#. F# is played by finger 1 on the E string. To play F, slide your first finger back toward the nut, leaving a small space between fingers 1 and 2.

F

1/2 step   whole step

Play "Whole or Half?" to hear the difference between F natural and F#.

Whole or Half?

Track 66

► Accidentals do not carry over the bar line. However, as a reminder, a cautionary accidental may be included as in measure 4.

The F major scale includes our new note F, and also B♭ from Lesson Seven. Note the B♭ in the F major key signature. This exercise uses quarter notes, then doubles the rhythm to eighth notes.

F Major Scale

Track 67

Continue to work on slurred bowing while practicing "F Major Arpeggio." Play slowly, and with excellent intonation.

Track 68

► Experiment by playing this with alternate bowings such as one bow per quarter note or two-then-one-bow for quarter notes.

F Major Arpeggio

Play the notes of "Lament" *pizzicato* until you become comfortable playing F natural. This tune should be played slowly, with long full bow strokes to portray its mournful character.

Track 69

Lament

Track 70

⁶⁄₈ Time Signature

One may think of ⁶⁄₈ time as having six beats to a measure, with an eighth note receiving one beat.

6   6 beats per measure
8   ♪ = 1 beat

Another way to count ⁶⁄₈ time is as two beats per measure, in other words, the dotted quarter note gets one beat.

6 or **2**
8   ♩.

Tap the rhythms in the examples below before playing them on the open strings. Count six beats per measure for slower tempos.

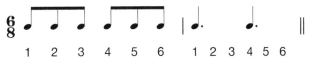

But you may wish to count two beats per measure for faster tempos.

Slow and Steady

Quick as a Wink

Count two beats per measure when you play "Oh, Dear, What Can the Matter Be?" Practice slurring three notes to a bow as marked.

Oh, Dear, What Can the Matter Be?

► When first learning a tune, you may start slowly, counting six beats to a measure, then change to two beats per measure as you play the tune faster.

"Irish Folk Song" is a slow tune with a touch of melancholy. Count six beats to each measure and play with a smooth legato bow.

Irish Folk Song

Sixteenth Notes

Track 75

Sixteenth Notes

Sixteenth notes are played twice as fast as eighth notes. Four sixteenth notes equal one quarter note. Sixteenth notes can be flagged or beamed. (Note: sixteenth notes will almost always be beamed together when in a group of two or four that start on the beat. Flags are used in more complex rhythms involving single sixteenth notes.)

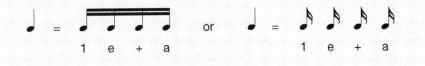

Clap and count the following sixteenth note rhythms in each song before playing them on your violin.

Track 76

Sweet Sixteen

Pretty Little Girl with the Red Dress On

American

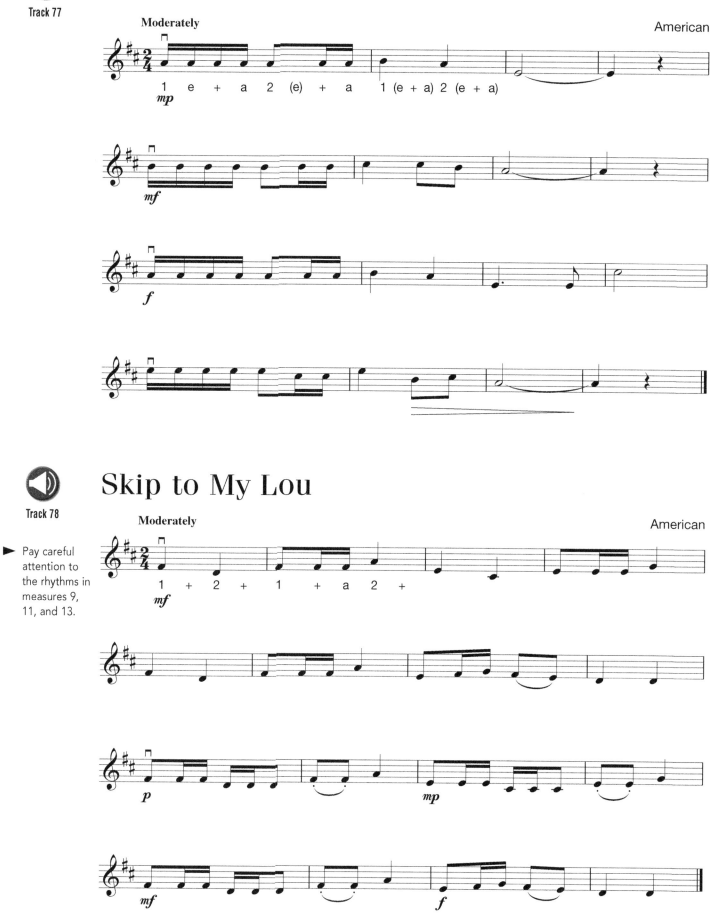

Skip to My Lou

American

▶ Pay careful attention to the rhythms in measures 9, 11, and 13.

"Cumberland Mountain Bear Chase" is an American folk song in the fiddle tradition. Tap the rhythm before playing and keep your bow strokes short on the sixteenth notes to give this tune plenty of dance-like energy.

Track 79

Cumberland Mountain Bear Chase

American

► In measure 12, lift your bow quickly after the quarter note.

A well-known tune from the Gold Rush era, the American folk song "Sweet Betsy from Pike" is played on the lower strings. Use lots of energy, and pay close attention to the dynamic markings throughout. Familiarize yourself with the key signature, time signature, and fingering. Play the tune *pizzicato* the first time through and *arco* the second.

Track 80

Sweet Betsy

American

Test Yourself!

Divide the following rhythms into measures according to the time signature given. Include a final double bar line at the end. Remember that the bottom number of the time signature determines which note receives one beat.

Once you've added bar lines, clap and count the rhythms and then play each example on your violin. You may first play the rhythms on one pitch of your choice. Then, improvise your own melody notes while playing the rhythms. Have fun and experiment!

The Basics

Track 81

Shifting

Shifting on a string instrument is moving your hand to different places on the fingerboard. Up until now your hand has stayed close to the scroll in what is called *first position*. Shifting allows you to extend the range of notes you can play on any one string, and also makes it easier to move between notes and strings. There are seven positions on the violin, but the most commonly used positions for intermediate violinists are first position and third position.

Track 82

Third Position on the D String

On the D string, prepare to play G with finger 3. Next, lightly slide your hand toward the bridge, so that finger 1 takes the place of finger 3. Now finger 1 will play G and you are in *third position*. Check your hand position with the diagrams in this box illustrating G in first and third positions.

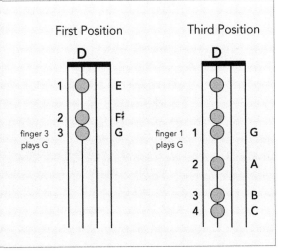

Moving finger 1 to third position allows you to play higher notes on the D string. Shifts/positions are marked with Roman numerals. Try shifting to third position in "Ready, Set, Shift!"

Track 83

Ready, Set, Shift!

► Listen carefully to make sure the two Gs in measures 2 and 3 are in tune with each other.

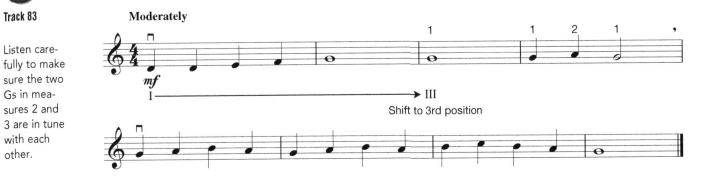

Track 84

Third Position on the A String

Shifting to third position is the same for each string: finger 1 takes the place of finger 3. On the A string, play D with finger 3. Now shift finger 1 toward the bridge to play D. You've found third position!

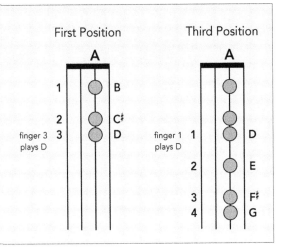

"Night Shift" starts in first position on the A string, shifts to third position, and then shifts back to first position.

Track 85

Night Shift

As we come to the end of *Play Violin Today! Level 2* we conclude with two solos and a duet to showcase the new skills and musical concepts you've learned along the way. We hope you continue to enjoy playing the violin and keep building on the foundation you've acquired!

The lovely Welsh folk song "Ash Grove" has the musical form AABA. Compare measures 1–8 with measures 9–16, and you will find they are exactly alike. Measures 17–24 form the contrasting B section, with the return of A from measures 25–32. A good way to practice "Ash Grove" is to work on the first A section alone, then the B section alone, playing the song from beginning to end when you have mastered the two sections individually.

Track 86

Ash Grove

A

"Minuet" is from *French Suite VI* by J.S. Bach. A classic dance from the Baroque period, the minuet is characterized by its $\frac{3}{4}$ meter and graceful style. Note the hooked bowing as marked.

Track 87

Minuet

J.S. Bach

Track 88

Our final tune, "Shenandoah," is arranged for two violins. Part One plays the melody throughout. You could play this part as a solo. To play the duet, find a friend or teacher to play the second violin part with you, or play along with the recording (Track 89 features a demo of both violin parts while Track 90 only plays the violin two part). Learn the second violin part as well, so you can switch parts with your partner, or play along with the recording.

**Track 89
Demo**

**Track 90
Play-Along**

Shenandoah

Fingering Charts

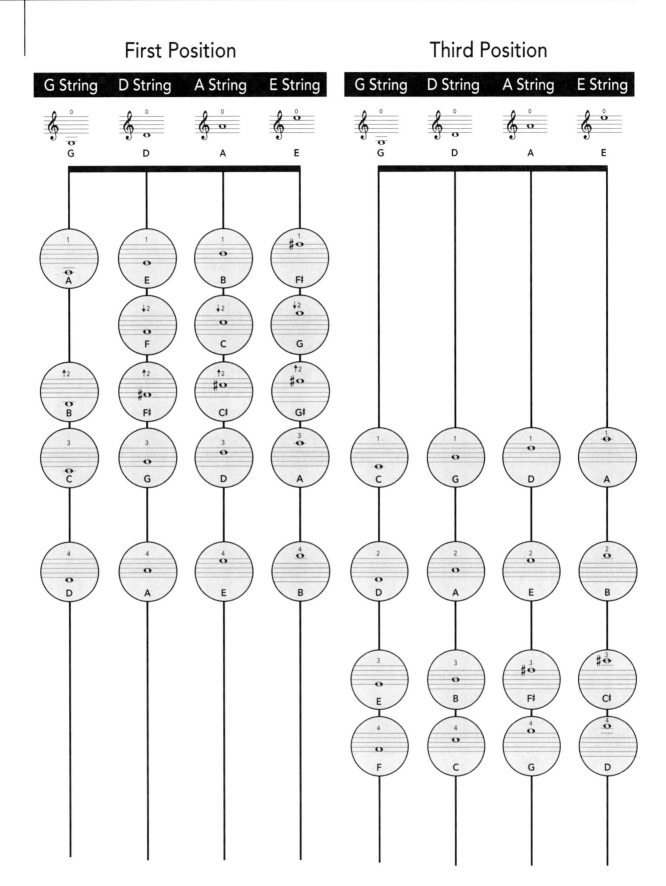

Glossary of Musical Terms

1st and 2nd ending	The 1st and 2nd ending signs are similar to the repeat sign. Play through the music until the repeat sign, playing the first ending. Then when repeating the music, go directly to the 2nd ending, skipping the music marked as "1st ending."
Arco	Play using the bow
Arpeggio	The notes of a chord played in succession, one note at a time
Crescendo	Gradually grow louder
Decrescendo	Gradually grow softer
Down bow	Begin the bow stroke at the frog
Fermata	A sign indicating to play a note longer than its value
Forte	Loud
Half step	The smallest interval in Western music; on the piano, from one key to the very next key
Hooked bowing	Two or more notes bowed in the same direction, with a stop in between the notes
Interval	The distance between two pitches
Legato	Play in a smooth manner, slurred
Major scale	Eight notes in succession, with half steps between the third and fourth, and seventh and eighth degrees, whole steps between all the others
Mezzo forte	Moderately loud
Mezzo piano	Moderately soft
Minuet	A dance of French origin from the 1600s in 3/4 time
Piano	Soft
Pizzicato	Pluck the string
Shifting	On a string instrument, moving the left hand to different places on the fingerboard
Slur	A bowing indication to play two or more notes with a single bow stroke
Staccato	Play in a short, separated manner
Stopped bow	Play in a detached style, with a small space of silence between the notes
Up bow	Begin the bow stroke near the tip, moving toward the frog
Whole step	Two half steps, also called a "second"